Nose Boop's

A book of kindness

"Bee more Dog"

A Diary

Rupert the Dog

This Diary belongs to:

"Be your own inspiration everyday" – Rupert the Dog

All poems are original and written by me or my sister, she asked to have a couple of hers published, so I agreed for a small fee,(two weeks biscuits from her)

My dog's name is /are:

I rescued my dog's on- date:

My cat's name is/are:

I rescued my cat's on- date:

There is no love more pure than that of a pet, cherish your new friend and give them whatever they want, always, let them climb on the sofa, let them sleep in your bed, as they are now a family member, never abandon them, shout at them, neglect them, if you do then you are not worthy of that love. – Rupert the Dog

What is kindness?

Well for me it's helping my sister, Gobshite, finish her breakfast, as clearly, she can't eat it all herself!

Or, it is snuggling with Mummy when she is poorly or fed up, or even sometimes letting pigeon bastard who frequents my fence daily, live another day. Laugh all you like, I have been known in my time to take down a bird mid-flight! But that is another story, and not really one for this kindness book.

*coughs

So back to what is kindness... well it's a known fact that you lot, "humans" are not always so kind and so this book, is especially for those of you who need a lesson or two in "what is kindness" and how to be kind. It's not rocket science, but I can see why some of you would need educating!!

As my, Great Grandma Whiskey, used to say ...

"Wupert, (she couldn't pronounce her r's) Wupert, if you've got nothing nice to say, then say fuck all"

This was her, with her lover Pedro, they ran off together to join the circus, and she was a world-famous trapeze artist.

Kindness ran through her veins, and she was full of quotes, another famous one of hers she'd say was "Do all things with kindness, you fucker" That was my Great Grandma Whiskey, tough as old boots, but heart of gold, if you tried to upset her, she'd bite your fucking nose off, give her a biscuit though and you'd gain a friend for life.

So back to kindness, the dictionary defines it as a quality, for being gentle, caring and helpful. However, not everyone (humans that is) possess these qualities, I for one cannot understand this, as it's within our nature to be kind, we are born kind (dogs). I think all humans are born kind, but I they lose their way as they grow, and their surroundings disables the quality.

Kindness doesn't have to be an elaborate act, in fact most acts of kindness are the simple ones that people remember the most.

My Mummy is kind, she takes care of me and my sister, and looks after Dad, but also takes care of Nanny Hammy and Grandad Potato, now for those of you who don't know who they are, well, they are my Mummies, Mom and Dad, and they live with us, in an extension on the house.

Sometimes, me and my sister will go over to their side of the house, when Mummy and Daddy are out, they look after us, which is very kind, as you see my sister was a rescue, and doesn't like being left. But we didn't always get to go over to Nannies, as before we all lived together we used to live in a rented house, and sometimes we had to be left on our own, and well, let me tell you the story....

Gobshite, or her formal name Titch, came to live with us after Mummy and Daddy went to view her in the kennels and knew they couldn't leave her there.

But she was, shall we say, somewhat fucking mental, now I know what you are all thinking, she had a bad upbringing, was traumatised, was abandoned, yes, yes and yes, but still no excuse for eating shit and terrorising the postman!!!

But, over time I grew to love her, and understand her

fears, that was until one day, when we were left awaiting Mummies return, and a parcel delivery man came to the house........

Back then, we used to have netted curtains, it was when they were sort of acceptable, now they should be burnt, hideous things, anyway, parcel delivery man decided to peer through said netted curtains, on this particular day, and boy oh boy, do I wish he hadn't... Gobshite, leapt up onto the window sill, teeth barred, hackles up and shredded the netted curtains, to the point they were literally just strips hanging from the rod!!!

I was aghast and shouted, what the fuck are you doing, Mummy is going to go mental, are you fucking crazy. She said, seeing the parcel delivery man triggered a memory and fear took over. I calmed her down and said, well not too worry, I am sure Mummy, will see the funny side!!!

Mummy came home, and did actually see the funny side, and in fact just brought new netted curtain, that was until Titch did the same thing again, not once, twice, or even three times, but four more times. We had blinds fitted in the finish, and a table put in front of the window to prevent Gobshite from jumping onto the window ledge!!!

But, Mummy, never batted an eyelid, never shouted, just each time brought new netted curtains, (fucking idiot) and placated Titch, and this people isn't kindness it's pure lunacy!! Joking.... of course it was a form of kindness!

So, back to now, we all live together, me, my sister, Mummy, Daddy and Nanny and Grandad, and in the main we rub along nicely, Mummy makes sure we are all fed and kept clean, especially Hammy, as she has a tendency to drop food down herself, like all the time, worse than me for gobbling her grub!! Oh, she's not like helpless, just a messy eater ha- ha

Daddy, is diabetic, type 2 and so Mummy has to make sure, he eats properly, I mean, yes he's a grown man, and no it's not really Mummies responsibility, but let's face it, men are fucking useless, when it comes to choosing the right food, so she cooks healthy meals, even I am on a grain free diet, but that's because you all know by now, I have allergies, and skin issues, which is just another thing Mummy has to care about, so you see, she is very kind and we love her.

It's not in grand gestures that forever love is found –
it's in the small daily endearments that grow the
heart.

Whether you are a dog lover cat lover or just simply
any animal lover, we come in all shapes and sizes,
and we all have different personalities, but one thing
we all share is the unconditional love we give time
after time.

Ball

I have a ball, I love it, and it is mine

Try to take it off me, and hear me pine

Every day I wake up, and I look for my ball

If I cannot find it, for sure you will hear me squawl

I will often drop it near your feet, then bark and shout

You think, you are in control then, of this no doubt

But the truth is, I am the one who is playing you

Therefore sometimes, I drop it, then pick it back up
too

Titch

Magic

A sprinkle for me, a sprinkle for you, magic sprinkled everywhere

You can't see it, you can't touch it, but know it's there

What could it be, I hear you say, is it dust or perhaps glitter

Oh, it's special and reserved for you, but not those who are bitter

I'll tell you shall I, what this magic is, yes please, I hear you cry

You can spread it too, give a little here, give a little there, and make a magic pie

It is kindness, simple as that, as kindness is magic, believe it or not

Makes everyone smile, makes everyone dance, magic inside your special spot

Notes:

Begging

We sit, we wait, patience is in our blood

We stare, we drool, waiting for that hot spud

Begging, is an art form, cats can't beat us at this game

We are masters, we are winners, we want all the fame

Any little morsal, any type of grub

We will sit there begging, we are in a club

Gimme, gimme, gimme, that tiny bit of toast

Or better still, what about that delicious pot roast

It doesn't matter what you've got, we sit there at your feet

Treading grapes, waiting eargley for any piece of meat

Kindness gives you the flutterbys in your belly -
Rupert the Dog

Always look for the positive in a day…. or food -
Rupert the Dog

January

Here again the fireworks damp, burnt out and left on the grass.

People sad, depressed and harassed.

It always seems a miserable month, dark and dreary.

Everyone, heads down feeling sad and very weary.

But you need to be more dog and live for the day.

Start seeing it as a new chapter and laugh I say.

It's only depressing if you make it so.

Get up and be happy, go with the flow.

Do something kind, smile and embrace the day.

As in thirty- one days it will soon be passed.

So fucking Cheer up and have a blast.

Mr Frosty

Ice, snow still on the ground

Look there, look all around

Remains to be seen, a carrot, a stone

Used to be someone now melting alone

A hat a scarf I was given one day

Now taken back not needed they say

Mr Frosty was my given name

Stood proud and tall I wanted the fame

Selfies took with me, laughter and smiles

Now just a memory a sad dirty pile

Rupert the Dog

January Birthday's & important dates

1st	19th
2nd	20th
3rd	21st
4th	22nd
5th	23rd
6th	24th
7th	25th
8th	26th
9th	27th
10th	28th
11th	29th
12th	30th
13th	31st
14th	
15th	
16th	
17th	
18th	

A dreary month for most, full of dark, cold days and for some making New Year's resolutions, that you never ever stick too, why bother, I say. You should be more dog, and say to yourself it's just another day, but one filled with opportunities for me to become a better person by random acts of kindness, talking of which………….

I remember once when I was just a pup, Dad had gone to do manly things, and Mummy and I were home alone!

She decided to mow the front lawn, however, didn't want to leave me inside on my own, so, came up with the genius concept of putting me in a washing basket with my lead tied to the tree!! Now, before you all start gasping and saying that was abuse, I was fine, I sat in the basket on a blanket and it was a mild day so didn't get too hot.

Mummy started mowing, it was an electric hover mower thing, and the lead was long. This turned out to be at Mummies peril, as she hadn't realised the lead had gotten caught under the mower and the next thing, she'd mowed over it and the dam thing cut out!

Now I can all hear you thinking, oh god! Did I jump out of the basket to save her, did I fuck, I sat there non- the wiser, snoozing, that was until Mummy went to bend down to pick the lead up!!!!!!!

Now call it what you like, intervention, a guardian angel, fate, luck, whatever but just as she was about to do this, the next door neighbour came out, and he must have seen or judged what had happened and shouted incredibly loud "NOOOOOOO" at Mummy, she jumped back, and I barked in fright and flung myself out of the basket and it upended and landed on me, making me stuck underneath!!

The neighbour, Bob, said "bloody hell, you would have been brown bread", (dead) he was neither from London or a cockney, ha! I just thought that sounded funnier ha-ha.

He went on to say, that Mummy would have been electrocuted and to never touch live wires, he then proceeded to turn the power off at the mains, helped me out from under the basket, and then he went the extra mile.

Mummy was crying, and saying that Dad would be upset, so Bob, not only finished mowing the lawn with his mower, he repaired our mower all before Daddy got home.

This, people, was an act of kindness like no other, he saved Mummies life, and was a hero, and when Daddy eventually got home, and Mummy relayed the story, he was so grateful to Bob, he took him a bottle of wine round, although this was not nearly enough for saving me from under the basket!!!

So, we can be kind in many ways, small, big, elaborate, whatever, but I want to impart my wisdom onto you to how you can become kind every day without even realising.

Kindness is king, you should wake every-day and think what act of kindness I shall do today. It's a smile, its saying hello to a stranger in the street, it's even, helping someone cross the road, like Mummy does with me, as I have absolutely no fucking road sense what so ever.

That is what kindness is.

So, have a plan, have attainable goals, and above all little steps, I mean I've got no fucking choice, with the little steps bit, ha! But what I mean is don't go out all gung-ho, as you'll fall at the first hurdle, also don't give yourself unrealistic goals, kindness comes in many forms, so start small.

I'm hoping by the end of your journey you'll feel happier, more relaxed and above all KINDER!! Not everyone has this natural ability, not everyone is a ray of fucking sunshine or happy, but I'm hoping by reading this they soon will be.

I believe in the magic of kindness

February

Amour

I saw you in the park

I wanted to be your friend

I tunnelled my snout

Up your non, barking end

Together we chased each other around

I then rolled over onto the ground

Submissive and coy wanting you to lick me

Barking sweet nothings about balls and wee

Rupert the Dog

Waiting

One woof, two woofs, three woofs, more

I love you my Mummy, I shall wait at your door

I will sit patiently until you come home

I shall lie on my blanket with my chewy bone

Ark, I hear you pulling into the drive

Boy I am excited can't wait for you to arrive

Wagging my tail, so happy with glee

Home you are its just you and me

Rupert the Dog

Remember, its only 11 months until Christmas!! Why not this year, give to an animal charity instead of buying useless crap for all the family, which they won't appreciate anyway. You can start by stock piling dry food, for dogs and cats throughout the year, then you can send them to your nearest rescue centre, they will really appreciate that. Mummy does this, and it makes her feel, good, and I help by sniffing the packages and giving them my seal of approval!!

If everyone did one act of kindness every day to help sad animals, the world would be a better place. So, January is done, look forward and feel energised and positive that you are doing something great. With each new day, your heart will grow, your smile will remain, and your life will feel enriched.

You could even go one step further and if in a position to do so adopt a furry best friend from your nearest shelter, cat or dog, (but dog) let love into your life, but I must stress, if you are serious about on embarking on this journey, then please answers these questions with candour, only then can you decide to adopt a dog or cat.

I will walk my new friend every day, at least twice a day, if capable (sometimes elderly dogs suffer with their joints)

If a cat, I will provide a safe environment if a house cat, or not live by a busy main road if they are allowed out

I will not leave my new friend alone for long periods of time

I will leave fresh water out every day, and feed him/her every day

I will play with my new friend for at least 20 minutes every day and love them #

I will provide a cosy bed, whether that be mine or the couch or their own

I will give them toys, to amuse themselves

I will not shun them if other (human) friends come round, but include them, as this is their home now

I will not worry about fur being on my furniture or clothes

I appreciate that you might stare at me when I am eating, or just when I am watching TV, I am ok with this

I will understand when you are poorly, I will have to take you to the Vet and it will cost money, maybe lots of money that is ok

I know you might sometimes, bark, or meow, and sometimes you might want attention all the time, I am ok with this

I know you might sometimes, chew things you shouldn't or have an accident on the carpet, with vomit or poop or wee, I am ok with this

I know you might sometimes get me up in the night for a wee or because you want to be sick, I am ok with this

I know that this is a big commitment and is sometimes harder than looking after a child

Even after knowing all of this, I am still prepared to adopt you, love you, never give you back, and commit to you for your life.

If human you can honestly answer yes to all of the above and understand all of the above, then I feel you are ready to adopt a new family member....so what are you waiting for.....

Nose Boop's

Nose boops, are my favourite thing

They lift your spirits, make your heart sing

When you are sad and feeling blue

This is when I come and nose boop you

I am always here, dark days and more

Soft, and furry with my soft little snore

There is no better love, than that from me

Best friend, companion, and nose boops for free

Rupert the Dog

February Birthday's & Important dates

1st	14t
2nd	15th
3rd	16th
4th	17th
5th	18th
6th	19th
7th	20th
8th	21st
9th	22nd
10th	23rd
11th	24th
12th	25th
13th	26th
	27th
	28th

February the month of love and fucking commercial crap from card sellers! Mummy and Daddy never bother with valentine's cards as they know how much they love each other already, I mean I constantly hear Mummy shouting endearments at Daddy, just the other day she yelled "take the fucking rubbish out will you, lazy fucking twat", can't get more romantic than that!!!

But seriously kindness and love costs nothing, it makes other humans feel good, it brings warmth and a general feeling of well- being.

I understand not everyone is good with feelings, and so you don't have to extol all of yours onto another person or hound them (ha, hound!) into participating in something they might not want too, I mean just a simple "good morning" a please , a thank you, a good weekend, these are pleasantries and you may only want a good morning back and not song and verse, but it's called human interaction, it's called being kind, which can make the world of difference to someone.

Being kind is free, being kind makes you a better person, being kind, should come as simple as breathing. If you are not a kind person, then you are a twat!!

Mummy used to work for a firm that every day for 3 years she'd walk into the office, happy, regardless of whether she wasn't or not, as it was her view it wasn't her colleague's problem if she'd had a shit weekend!

Anyway, I digress, everyday she'd walk in and say good morning, and one person, not once, never did she ever say good morning without being prompted, never even used to turn around in her seat, look up, or utter a word back, it was soul destroying, rude and uncomfortable.

Now, this person could've been having issues at home, issues at work, issues with Mummy, but a simple morning, how are you, COSTS NOTHING, PEOPLE! So, any miserable fuckers reading this, if you are that person who doesn't even acknowledge your colleagues, regardless of who you think you are, people are people, with emotions, feelings and depth, and it is rude and unkind, so change your ways, as of today. It's simple, a smile, a good morning, a, hope you have a good day today, makes for a whole different way to start the day, not only does it make that person feel good, it brings happiness, which in turn leads to kindness. So, do it. Don't be a TWAT for the rest of your life.

You know it's easy to think you are kind, you may be reading this and saying to yourself, well I am a kind person, but ask yourself this, if you saw someone crying alone on a bench, would you approach that person, or walk on by thinking Oh, that's not my problem or I haven't got time for this shit today? Kindness would be to stop ask and if they are ok, it might make all the difference, me I'd snuggle them, and let them stroke my belly, but you don't need to do that as you might get arrested ha!

"Don't ever think you are above someone, or presume you are better than them. Everybody has a back story, and we are ALL on a journey. Make sure on yours you extend a smile, some kindness and love" – Rupert the dog

No act of kindness, no matter how small, is ever wasted.

Postie

I sit and wait every day, in my chair, and I watch for
you

I know when you are coming, I see the bag of blue

My hackles start to rise, and I find myself barking

I cannot help myself as I see you embarking

You trundle down our driveway, with your stupid
sack of mail

I am now going mental, barking and shouting, I need
to exhale

I am now at the front door, ready to strike

Mummy fast behind me, shouting you little tyke

Too late, I've got it, ripped it to shreds

Mummy standing behind me shaking her head

Oh Postie, Postie why do you have to come,

Every day it's the same, ruining my fun

Titch

March

Mrs Bumble

Mrs Bumble bee exhausted and worn out.

I see you there on my patio I began to shout.

Mummy came to see what all the fuss was about.

She then spied you too and knew immediately what
to do.

Off she went to fetch sugar and water, Never Honey!
For you.

She dropped a tiny amount on the floor and gently
you lapped it up.

We could see the transformation it was a wonder to
behold.

It wouldn't be long now said Mummy before it took
hold.

And so, it was true within a moment's grace.

Up you buzzed with a smile on your face.

Rupert the Dog

So, spring has sprung, and you feel lighter and happier. The Birds are chirruping and tweeting, and flowers are blooming, and it's time to embrace the milder weather and longer brighter days.

Talking of tweeting, you can follow me at @ruperttitch if you don't already, and see what acts of kindness I get up to on a regular basis, I also have the best followers and friends and with their support I raise money for a charity called Wetnose Animals, they are a small not-for-profit organisation staffed by dedicated volunteers and they work tirelessly to help sad animals.

Some of my best friends, regularly help my efforts in raising money and I want to acknowledge some of them by saying you guys Lubly Lu, Seamus, Falkor, Ziggy, Stan, Kerri, Lily Bean and Ollie you have all been amazing, and it's their acts of kindness over the past year that have helped and encouraged me. I love you all very much.

So, you see, kindness takes shape in many forms, I try to raise a smile for my many followers, as even this can make a big difference to someone's day, but it's helping sad animals that really fills me with joy.

When I wrote my first book, it was because I was inspired to try and raise funds for animals that's how it all started by writing Diary of a Fat Jack Russell and sending some of my royalties from every book sold to Wetnose and from there it grew as did my followers.

But of course, I understand and appreciate that not everyone is, able to raise funds, but even donating food to animal's shelters, or simply retweeting information for dogs or cats or any animal in need, it highlights the charity it highlights the need and that is better than doing nothing.

Every Act of Kindness grows the spirit and

strengthens the soul

That sound!

Nothing gets you moving faster, than hearing that
sound
Retching, retching, retching, then oh god don't look
around

There on the new rug, a big steaming pile of vom
Me I want to eat it, give it me, nom nom nom

You are shouting and screaming in such a high
pitched voice
Yelling at me to stop it, but I can't it tastes so nice

It's got bits of grass in it, after I went outside to forage
I must've eaten something yum, but I'm sure it wasn't
porridge

Maybe it was a snail, a wiggly worm, or even my
fave, fox pooh
But whatever I gobbled up, it didn't agree with me
nor my bottom too

March Birthday's & Important Date's

1st

2nd

3rd

4th

5th

6th

7th

8th

9th

10th

11th

12th

13th

14th

15th

17th

18th

19th

20th

21st

23rd

24th

25th

26th

27th

28th

29th

30th

31st

Kindness is king

Walking to the shops one day, I spied you struggling
but you wouldn't say

Many people passed you by, not a moment's notice
did I spy

I wondered how long it would be, before someone
would help me

If I were in the same situation, helpless, stuck it
wasn't always the case, but now in a rut

So, I walked up to the lady in the wheelchair, and said
hey, "Can I help you there"

A smile, a nod, a moment of being bold

I helped the lady over the busy road

A few minutes out of my life, but for her, one less
moment of strife

Kindness is king and makes the world go around

Not dollars or pennies or even pounds

And so, April is here, a cliché month, as they say it's always rains, but even the rain can be good, you should dance in the rain at least once, try it, let it wash over you and feel its soft splashing rivulets drip down your face. What harm can it do, my Great Grandad Alfred used to say, "Can only get wet once son"

Great Grandad Alfred was a strong feisty dog, but stubborn as anything, that's why Great Grandma Whiskey ran off, as he never wanted to do anything. He would lie most days in front of the fire, dreaming of the days he chased rabbits down holes, but he was a good kind old boy, and he used to let me share his biscuits.

I think I must get my handsome looks from him, same colouring. I remember once when I was just a pup, we were out walking the farmer's field, and there running free was a dog who looked just like my Great

Grandad Alfred, but of course it wasn't him as he had died, some years before, anyway, it shocked Mummy, and she started calling after this dog, but of course he wouldn't come, so I tried to help, by barking, and this dog, stopped dead in his tracks, turned and looked at me, and barked back. Mummy then gently coaxed him over and we could see he had a collar, but no tag.

Mummy was scared he was lost, and so held onto his collar, and walked him all the way back to our home, with me on the lead beside her, it was very difficult, as Mummy had to kind of walk with a crouch, but as she is small and stumpy like me, so it wasn't too bad!! Ha

She let me, in and then called the nearest vets, and they said to bring him in and they could check for a microchip. So, Mummy, bundled him in the car, and said to me be a good boy, I won't be long, and off she went to take him. Turned out he was lost, and he was microchipped, he had escaped out of his garden, and his owners were fraught, but so thankful to Mummy. And that people, is another act of kindness, Mummy didn't give it a second thought to help that doggy, didn't fear he may be snappy, didn't fear he might bite her, although I would've protected her!! It was second nature to her, to help him.

You would think kindness should be the same as breathing, comes naturally, and without it you can't survive...but sadly not. I find it hard to comprehend how humans can hunt, torture, abandon or mistreat any animal.

What drives them, are they wired different? I mean when you look at humans, you are all basically the same, made up of flesh, bones, hair and teeth and yet you are all so very, very different. If only it were that simple that we could flick a switch and make all humans kind.

Naive, I know, but to me being kind is simple, loving other animals is easy, helping others comes naturally, and so why, oh, why can't all humans follow suit, why can't they see that hunting beautiful animals, will lead to their extinction.

And how can any human hurt an innocent defenceless dog or cat is beyond me. How can bullfighting still be legal in this day and age, what pleasure is that seeing an innocent defenceless animal tortured to death.....are all the people that fill the stadium to watch this horrendous show, filled with no compassion whatsoever.. take out the fact that they call it tradition, it's cruel, it's wrong, surely you can see that, an animal has emotions, trust me, and it feels pain, so why is this still allowed.

So many horrendous acts of torture and killing take place against animals, too many for me to mention, and to be honest to painful, it fills my heart with sorrow every day that humans have been stripped of the kindness gene, have allowed their surroundings, to mould them into monsters, it sickens me, but all we can do is keep fighting the good fight.

No more

The floor is hard, cold and damp, I'm left alone in this concrete prison

People come, people go, and some look and then walk on by like I'm a villain

The days are long, all I want is a family, I sit by the gate, hope on my face

In they walk, a couple hand in hand, so I get up and I start to pace

Have they seen me, I'm sure I look cute, so what if my teeth are wonky

And I have gangly legs and who cares I'm nearly as tall as donkey

All I know is I can't take no more, no more rejection, no more sorrow

I just want a cosy bed and a blanket and not one I must borrow

You see, being a rescue dog isn't easy, we have been forgotten about

We are left, because nobody cared, abandoned and abused, kicked out

Oh, they are coming closer to my cage, maybe today is my day, my dream

They look kind and smiley and they smell of cookies and cream

Oh, the joy, no more will I snooze, on concrete or damp or alone in a cage

I've been chosen, it's true I'm off to pastures new, where I can live till old age

Rupert the Dog

Back to April, and the, flowers are starting to bloom, the sky is looking bluer and the trees have leaves on them again. Talking of trees, I absolutely love, love, love trees, the aroma they give off, and then of course you can circle them, try and jump up them, and then pee up them ha-ha! Of course this is my favourite part….oh come on….I am dog it's what we do… Oh also they harbour squirrel bastards, now don't get me wrong, I couldn't eat a whole one, but those bushy tailed little fuckers, love to taunt me. I have a special squirrel squeal, it's rather hi pitched and makes Mummy laugh every time she hears it. Of course, I know it makes her laugh, so I do it even more, as laughter is the best medicine for everyone. You all should try and laugh at least once a day, or make someone else laugh, it is good for the soul.

"A Kind and compassionate act is often its own reward"

April Birthday's & Important dates

1st

2nd

3rd

4th

5th

6th

7th

8th

9th

10th

11th

12th

13th

14th

15th

16th

17th

18th

19th

20th

21st

22nd

23rd

24th

25th

26th

27th

28th

29th

30th

Cats V Dogs

So, cats, you think you are so superior and smarter than us

But, think again you bag of fur balls, as we are kings so thus

We can learn new tricks, and are loyal through and through

All you are interested in is napping, snoozing, and bidding us adieu

We have an amazing sense of smell, and are masters at the chase

You cats just sit around, and really are just a waste of space

You don't even know how to bark, even though you do a hundred different sounds

All we hear when you meow is the wiry concord that mine ear confounds

So it is proven Dogs rule ok, we are better than Cats, that is what I say

Ha- ha Anon ....

- Written maybe by Rupert!

Mr Worm

I went a walking on a sunny day

Blue skies all around me, with fields of hay

There upon the path in front of me

Struggling in the heat

Was a plump worm for all to see?

I crouched down to be near him

And I gently placed in my hand

I took him to the field, the green lush land

I didn't want him to be eaten on this hot day

So, this was an act of kindness that led me on my way

Rupert the Dog

Hump it

There is something in my genes, that makes me feel
frisky
I think it's because I'm dog and not down to Great
Grandma Whisky

Even though I've had the snip, I still get the urges
Sometimes I will Hump my sister even though she
curses

When I was younger I'd Hump my toy teddy
But he got all sticky and I didn't like him in my beddy

Now I don't Hump as much, too old and arthritic for
all that
But sometimes the old spark will set me off, even
though I'm too fat

I'm like an old grumpy furry tortoise, struggling to
get it on
But it soon passes and the feeling leaves me, then it's
gone

Rupert the Dog

May Birthday's & important dates

1st	19th
2nd	20th
3rd	21st
4th	22nd
5th	23rd
6th	24th
7th	25th
8th	26th
9th	27th
10th	28th
11th	29th
12th	30th
13th	31st
14th	
15th	
16th	
17th	

May, a month of merriment, the flowers are in full bloom, everyone is feeling more refreshed, longer days, sunshine and laughter. We can all sometimes, forget our neighbours, people in need, the horrors of the world, it can be exhausting I know.

But, to be truly kind, means that you wear it like a skin, its second nature to you, it is part of who you are. I want to hi- light something that is happening in Indonesia, something you may already be aware of, but it needs bringing to your attention again.

Palm Oil! The World's most widely consumed vegetable oil. It is often just an ingredient listed in small type on many labels. But its human and environmental costs are enormous.

The production of palm oil is having a devastating effect on the planet, especially Indonesia. In 2015 an epic and horrendous fire swept through the forests, they were drained to make way for palm oil plantations. Many people died, but so did thousands of orangutans. It's these graceful beautiful great apes that I want to bring to the forefront of your mind.

They are endangered, and many are being left orphaned as man, ploughs on through their natural habitat, all so you can eat Nutella on Toast!! It's absurd, and action needs to be taken

There are many organisation's already trying to do something, Rainforest Rescue is just one organisation trying to make a difference. If you can spare five minutes out of your busy day, please visit their website

www.rainforest-rescue.org and read up on the horrors of palm oil, and what you can do to help save the Orangutans. Thank you.

Kind Words, Kind Thoughts, Kind Deeds

June

Stallone

We used to see him every day, walking his dog nod
and smile, hello he would say.

Then we saw him less, his shoulders turned down, his
doggy was not well, he said with a frown

Then came the day out alone he was walking, not
even a nod, not even know talking.

We got news that his dog was sadly put to sleep, oh
god did we feel sad, oh god did we weep

We didn't see him for many, many, days, worried and
concerned we had to say.

So, popped round his house but no one was in, we left
a note pushed through his front door

Wanting to say we were worried and more

Then out of the darkness and sad awful weeks, there was our neighbour walking the streets.

He stopped and said he had gotten the note, and how he was glad to know people cared,

He was so very sad he lost his best friend his life he shared

But now he was feeling less lost and alone

He had adopted a new friend, everyone meet Stallone

Rupert the Dog

Doggy farts

Jesus Christ I hear you yell, what the fuck hell is that smell
Mummy blames Dad, he looks disgusted, that is not me he shouts, the injustice

I lie between them, snoring away, letting out farts, stinky as decay
Oh the smell is such a wonderful aroma, rotten and rancid, puts you in a near coma

Nothing beats the smell of my bum, I often think, ooo yum yum

Rupert the Dog

Kindness Quotes

A bucket full of kindness is better than a bucket full of shit - Great Grandma Whiskey

Never think you are better than another, we are all on a road of discovery, some roads though are long, some glittered with gold, and some cracked, but each road in the end leads to the same destination, so just remember to be kind - Rupert the Dog

Kindness in the end wins – Rupert the Dog

Kindness is not to brag, you fucking little show off, but to just do – Great Grandma Whiskey

So, some people don't like dogs, some people, like some dogs, and some people are just dicks! I mean what's not to like about any dog really. Oh, I hear some saying well, it's because they had a bad experience, or it was a nippy little bastard or it was a bad breed and attacked someone.

Well let's get something straight, there's no such thing as a bad breed, just a bad owner, i.e. humans. Example, when a baby is born it does not come out of the womb yelling expletives, or wielding a knife, no, it's born innocent, and then it's, surroundings and upbringing teach it right from wrong, if then said baby becomes a killing murderous bastard, then it's down to what it's been taught.

Now the same applies to dogs, when a puppy pops out of his Mummy, it doesn't then rear up and rip the face off the nearest human, nor does it attack for no apparent reason, puppies are innocent bundles of joy, whether that be a Cockapoo, Jack Russell, Rottweiler, Labrador, Pitbull or French bulldog, too many to keep mentioning, but you get the gist, no Dog is born vicious!

Man, and surroundings all mould the dog and it reacts to its environment. Dogs don't have a voice, like humans, we can't say "please stop that, it's annoying me" so eventually we bark, then we bite, but then of course we are labelled a bad dog.

All dogs, can become feisty, and you should never ever leave us unattended with babies, children or cats!! As we can sometimes, like humans reach a point of no return when prodded or poked often enough, this doesn't make us evil, it makes us emotional, as yes we have emotions, we love, we serve, we befriend, we honour, we give day after day, unconditionally and all we ask for in return is a warm loving safe home.

It truly breaks my heart, to know of my fellow canines, who suffer at the hands of cruel humans every single day, whilst I'm writing this many are being beaten, abandoned, eaten, yes eaten, at a hideous festival called Yulin, which was brought to my attention by Ricky Gervais, you should follow him on Twitter, if you don't already, as he is an amazing advocate and voice for sad animals especially dogs, just don't tell Ollie, his cat!!!!

Please Stop

To all you hunters, hunting for pleasure and sport
I beg you, I urge you Please stop, no more, I'm
fraught

Can't you see animals have feelings, with every right
to survive
What gives you the right to shoot them, please stop,
keep them alive

They soon will be extinct, wiped out from our earth
Yet, like you, me and everyone else have been here
since birth

Please stop, why, oh, why must you do it, it's not too
late
Hunting is cruel, evil and wrong, it only fills people
with hate

You must have compassion, animals have souls and a
heart
Please stop the killing, the murdering too, you are
tearing them apart

Rupert the Dog

June Birthday's & Important dates

1st	16th
2nd	17th
3rd	18th
4th	19th
5th	20th
6th	21st
7th	22nd
8th	23rd
9th	24th
10th	25th
11th	26th
12th	27th
13th	28th
14th	29th
15th	30th

Kindness makes you the most beautiful person in the world no matter what you look like

July is upon us, long hot days, barbecues, beach trips, and sunburn, and lots of fucking idiots, who walk around without their tops on, all pasty skin and blubber, listen people, nobody looking to see that, cover up, think of the damage you are doing to your skin for starters, and then to my eyes.

Then there are also the imbeciles who still think its ok to leave dogs in hot cars, WHAT IS WRONG WITH YOU PEOPLE! if you are one of the fucking twats reading this now who really thinks its ok to leave your dog in the car even for just one minute, then let me tell you fuck face it is NOT, ever, never, and to make the point hit home, I want you to put on a fleece, go on, do it, then on the hottest day, maybe that's today whilst you are reading this, go and sit in your car, take this book with you.

Right, dickhead are you in the car? yes, well zip up that fleece, **do not turn** the engine on, shut all the windows and now sit there for however long you can stand it, I am guessing already you are starting to feel uncomfortable, as the car will be baking already, after about just 2 minutes you will start to sweat, but you see the difference is you actually can sweat out of your skin, me being dog don't have that ability, I have to sweat out of my paws and as I am stuck in this baking prison, its proving rather difficult.

I am sure by now if you have continued with this experiment you are very hot and uncomfortable, but now you can open the door take off the fleece and get some air, me I don't have thumbs and my fur is my skin, so again I am pretty much fucked, and at this point I am seriously on the verge of death, yes in about another 10 minutes my organs will start to shut down and boil, thanks to you, you fucking selfish idiotic mindless twat.

If I have managed to get the message across, just how insane it is to NEVER leave a dog or any pet for that matter in a car on a hot day, then please pass this message on as we need to still educate complete and utter morons!

Thank you

July

Just a Minute

A hot sweltering day, the sun is beating down,
making some people angry, causing them to frown,

That's because it's roasting, uncomfortable and hot,
they are stuck in work like being boiled in a lobster
pot

And then there is me, took to the shops, left in the car,
you said, "don't worry I am not going far"

But a minute ticks by and the heat inside the car has
risen, and now I've started to pant stuck in this hot
prison.

Now 5 minutes has gone by and still no sign of you, I
am really starting to stress, and my heart is racing too,

It is now so hot in the car that my breath is laboured,
I hope you come back soon, and free me from this
scorching cocoon.

A few minutes that's all anyone ever said, but trust me that's all it takes for me to be dead, I've literally been boiled alive, no escape, no way out

I cannot even shout, and all because you thought I would be ok, even though it is a boiling hot day.

Rupert the Dog

DON'T BE A FUCKING TWAT, NEVER LEAVE YOUR DOG IN THE CAR ON A HOT DAY!

July Birthday's & Important Date's

1st

2nd

3rd

4th

5th

6th

7th

8th

9th

10th

11th

12th

13th

14th

15th

16th

17th

1

19th

20th

21st

22nd

23rd

24th

25th

26th

27th

28th

29th

30th

31st

August

Ice-cream

That time of year, you could hear the cheer

The chimes of the van it was the ice-cream man

All the kids lined up patiently in the street

Mums, Dads, watching, tapping their feet

Oh the joy, what should I choose,

Shall it be the whipped one with a flake, or the one called a rocket

I stand there lingering jangling the money in my pocket

The decision got harder the longer I looked, I wanted them all

But secretly I coveted the one I wasn't allowed and that was the screwball

August, half way through the year, give yourself a

cheer! What acts of kindness, if any have you accomplished? The summer is a time we can easily forget animals in need, as the sun is shining, holidays are in full swing and everyone is carefree, but try and spare a thought for animals in the heat, give plenty of water, keep them cool and in the shade.

Mummy, always makes sure, me and my sister are kept cool in the summer months, we have a fan, a sail outside that gives shade, and she puts ice in our water bowl, as last year was particularly hot, some days it reached 92F which is very hot especially for dogs, as we have lots of fur, and sweat out of our paws, like I said earlier on.

I remember one year, we were having another hot summer (one week) HA! The, U.K is renowned for not really having heat waves, and when we do, it makes the news, and reporters always say, its hotter than Jamaica, fucking idiots! Anyway, it was baking, and me being slightly tubby and very furry, was panting and didn't know what to do with myself, which was until Mummy, came up with the genius concept of shaving me!!!!

Now, let me tell you, there is photographic evidence, but they will NEVER see the light of day, as I looked like something from a fucking horror movie, for starters, she decided to do it herself!! *Owners, never ever try and shave your dog yourself and secondly, it was with a beard trimmer, not actual dog clipper!!! FFS …

I was held in a head lock, as the noise of the buzzing, terrified me, whilst Mummy placated me with a soothing voice, saying its ok son! NO IT WAS NOT WOMAN!! .. She shaved some of the fur off, but because I kept wriggling, parts were shaved so close to the skin, I was completely bald, then other parts were left with tufts. I shall NEVER forgive her, well that's a lie, ok it took me all like 3 minutes, and a biscuit, but fuck off, it was horrendous.

I looked like I had been in a fight with Edward Scissor Hands, the shame was awful, I couldn't go out for a week, as all the dogs on the estate, just started laughing, every time they saw me, and then the worst was Ginger Bastard, the next doors cat, that evil little fucker, shouted, HA HA What happened fatso, did you finally explode out of your fur, That little twat!!

So, the moral of the story, take us to a reputable dog groomer, and do not be like my Mummy the fucking idiot..

*love you Mummy

So, the rug rats and snot infested petri dishes have broken up from school, and probably already doing you're fucking head in! Well, good job you have this book then, as being the kind fellow I am, I have some splendid activities for you and your little fuckers.

First, teach them, patience, manners, and kindness, these are free, you can do this by making them sit for hours, doing absolutely fuck all, until they shout I'M BORED, or you can take them out to a wooded area, armed with a bag, a list of items they are to collect and make them search for the golden egg!!

Of course, you, should've boiled an egg until hardboiled, then painted gold without them seeing, and you should have hidden said egg, along the way! The list of items that they must search for can be a leaf shaped like a feather, or a stone shaped like a heart, or a twig, etc., you get the gist, use items on the list that you would find in a wooded area, or park if you don't live near any wooded areas! Then each child has a bag, and you shout what to find, the one who comes across the golden egg is the winner, and is rewarded with a YAY, you found the egg, ha, joking you can reward them how you like, just don't make it too elaborate, as you want them to know the best things in life are free!! - Your welcome

Another activity you can indulge in that costs nothing, is Pirates, make them a hat from a piece of newspaper, (it is simple really, watch You Tube) then again search for the missing treasure, either in the house or around the garden. Make sure you have hidden a box of old jewels or coins somewhere. Now send them off with clues to find the hidden treasure.

These activities, promote team work, teach patience and above all, give you at least an hour's grace, from the whiny little fuckers!!

The summer months, are for dogs to laze around, cats to snooze all day, it's a month of holidays and feeling free, some of the best things in life, never overlook the small gestures or take them for granted, a smile can change a person's day so always pass it on, hugs can change a life and just sometimes listening when someone wants to be heard can make all the difference.

Stop, Look and Listen, make this your new mantra #SLL

STOP – and give someone a smile

LOOK – to see how you can help someone

LISTEN- to that friend, relative, older person or teenager – we all need to be heard sometimes.

Help people, who are less fortunate than you, does not have to be grand gestures, it could be, offering to cut their grass, collect some shopping, or simply hearing them talk, give them the time, as there is always somebody worse off than you.

KINDNESS IS THE GREATEST GIFT YOU CAN GIVE

Interesting Dog Facts

- There are more than 150 dog breeds, divided into 8 classes: sporting, hound, working, terrier, toy, non-sporting, herding, and miscellaneous.

-

- According to a recent survey, the most popular name for a dog is Max. Other popular names include Molly,   Sam, Zach, and Maggie.

-

  - Dogs can vary in size from a 36 inch (150+ lb.) Great Dane to a 2 lb. Chihuahua.

  -

  - Puppies and kittens can be adopted as early as 8 weeks of age. Until then, they should stay with their moms and littermates.

  - About 1/3 of the dogs that are surrendered to animal shelters are purebred dogs.

  -

  - Contrary to popular belief, dogs do not sweat by salivating. They sweat through the pads of their feet.

  -

- Dogs may not have as many taste buds as we do (they have about 1,700 on their tongues, while we humans have about 9,000), but that doesn't mean they're not discriminating eaters. They have over 200 million scent receptors in their noses (we have only 5 million) so it's important that their food smells good and tastes good.

- The term "dog days" has nothing to do with dogs. It dates to Roman times, when it was believed that Sirius, the Dog Star, added its heat to that of the sun from July 3 to August 11, creating exceptionally high temperatures.

- Did you know they were female? Toto's role in The Wizard of Oz was played by a female Cairn terrier named Terry, and the Taco Bell dog is a female Chihuahua named Gidget.

  - Former US President Teddy Roosevelt had a Pit Bull named Pete.

  - An adult dog has 42 teeth.

- If a dog isn't spayed or neutered, a female dog, her mate and their offspring can product 67,000 dogs in 6 years.

- The most successful mountain rescue dog ever was a St Bernard named Barry, who lived during the early 1800's and saved 40 lives.

-

- It was recently discovered that dogs do see in colour, just not as vivid as we see.

-

- Nearly all but two breeds of dogs have pink tongues: the Chow Chow and the Shar-pei both have black tongues.

-

- The Poodle haircut was originally meant to improve the dog's swimming abilities as a retriever, with the pom-poms left in place to warm their joints.

- The top five favourite breeds of dogs in the US are: Labrador retriever, Golden Retriever, German shepherd, Beagle, and Dachshund. Note sure why the Jack Russell isn't in this list!!!

-

- The Basenji is the only bark less dog in the world.

-

- Greyhounds can reach a speed of up to 45 miles per hour.

-

- When a puppy is born, he is blind, deaf, and toothless.

-

- All dogs, regardless of breed, are direct descendants of wolves and technically of the same species. SO, I AM A WOLF ………

-

- A dog's whiskers — found on the muzzle, above the eyes and below the jaws — are technically known as vibrissae. They are touch-sensitive hairs than sense minute changes in airflow.

-

- Dogs can locate the source of a sound in 6/100ths of a second by using their swivelling ears like radar dishes.

Interesting Cat Facts

- Cats are one of, if not the most, popular pet in the world.

-

- There are over 500 million domestic cats in the world.

-

- Cats and humans have been associated for nearly 10000 years.

-

- Cats conserve energy by sleeping for an average of 13 to14 hours a day.

-

- Cats have flexible bodies and teeth adapted for hunting small animals such as mice and rats.

-

- A group of cats is called a clowder, a male cat is called a tom, and a female cat is called a molly or queen while young cats are called kittens.

-

- Domestic cats usually weigh around 4 kilograms (8 lb 13 oz) to 5 kilograms (11 lb 0 oz).

-
- The heaviest domestic cat on record is 21.297 kilograms (46 lb 15.2 oz).

-
- Cats can be lethal hunters and very sneaky, when they walk their back paws step almost exactly in the same place as the front paws did beforehand, this keeps noise to a minimum and limits visible tracks.

-
- Cats have powerful night vision, allowing them to see at light levels six times lower than what a human need in order to see.

-
- Cats also have excellent hearing and a powerful sense of smell.

-
- Older cats can at times act aggressively towards kittens.

-
- Domestic cats love to play, this is especially true with kittens who love to chase toys and play fight. Play fighting among kittens may be a way for them to practice and learn skills for hunting and fighting.

-
- On average cats live for around 12 to 15 years.

-
- Cats spend a large amount of time licking their coats to keep them clean.

-
- Feral cats are often seen as pests and threats to native animals.

-

Um, have you noticed how there are far more dog facts than cat facts – just saying!!

Whether you are a dog person or cat person ...each brings its own qualities, dogs are soothing and are often used for therapy, whereas cats have a certain superiority about them, and is often said that you don't own a cat they own you. But owning either is a gift and they should be cherished, always.

August Birthday's & Important Date's

1st	19th
2nd	20th
3rd	21st
4th	22nd
5th	23rd
6th	24th
7th	25th
8th	26th
9th	27th
10th	28th
11th	29th
12th	30th
13th	31st
14th	
15th	
16th	
17th	
18th	

September, a time to reflect where has the year gone so far, new terms, new beginnings, new starts for some. The leaves are turning into a beautiful array of golds, yellows and burnt reds and there is a crispness in the air, time for socks, pyjamas and cosy blankets at night, and that's just me!!

However, after the enjoyment of the holidays, humans can sometimes be insensitive and selfish, let us take a moment to think about the rubbish you leave behind, on beaches in the hedgerows, plastic cups, bottles, crisp packets, containers, all ruining our planet, humans too lazy to take it home or put it in the bin.

The devastation it is having on wildlife and mammals it's awful. You can do your bit, by stopping to pick up any bits of plastic you see, take it home recycle it, or put it in the appropriate bin, every little bit helps. Mummy did an experiment not too long back and went out armed with a bag, (re-useable) and just walked from our home to the shop and along the way she stopped to pick up any bits of rubbish she could see. When she got back it was shocking, the contents, were as listed below, and this was just in a two-mile radius!

4 x coffee cups!

4 x plastic drinks bottles

3 x cans

2 x straws

1 x carton from a very popular fast food place!

10 x crisp packets

2 x plastic rings (you find on beer cans)

3 x plastic carrier bags

All these were just discarded and strewn in the undergrowth along the path she walked, there no doubt would've been more, but she had filled her bag. Every day Mummy picks litter up off our street, where mindless selfish idiots have dropped it.. How lazy or inconsiderate are you to do that?

Wildlife suffers, and it's killing them, we are drowning in plastic, some might say it was the best invention, but I disagree and feel we should go back to re-useable, like when you had to take your pop bottles back!! Either way, we all need to think when buying items, to not just throw them in the street, take them home.

Every action has a re-action

September

Plastic

Plastic, plastic, everywhere, in hedgerows, on
beaches, just left for all to see

Nobody really caring, just off they flee

Littering our streets causing damage and harm

Many poor animals, sad but can't raise the alarm

That's down to you human, stopping to think

If you don't do something, we'll be on the brink

The damage of plastic is there for all to see

Awash with the stuff, suffocating your soul

Do something now, act, make it your goal?

Pick it up off the floor and put it in the bin

Or better yet take it home recycle win, win

Rupert the Dog

September Birthday's & Important Date's

1st	19th
2nd	20th
3rd	21st
4th	22nd
5th	23rd
6th	24th
7th	25th
8th	26th
9th	27th
10th	28th
11th	29th
12th	30th
13th	
14th	
15th	
16th	
17th	
18th	

KINDNESS IS SPREADING SUNSHINE INTO OTHER PEOPLE'S LIVES REGARDLESS OF THE WEATHER

October

There is a definitive chill in the air now, crisp sharp mornings, and darker nights, the month of October, where everyone gets excited for Halloween and then Christmas. But can we stop and spare a thought for the animal's that will be hibernating now, such as hedgehogs and take care to look out for them. If you see one out in the day then it is most likely injured, and needs assistance, so please take it to your nearest vets, or wildlife centre and they will know what to do.

I also want to bring to your attention the horrors that are happening to stray or lost dogs, who've ended up in government –run shelters and are being handed over to universities for use in experiments. And many of these poor animals are also being supplied to veterinary schools for student teaching.

It is mainly Brazil, but further investigations have found that USA, Canada and Australia are using these dogs for experiments. It is shocking and revolting to think that somebodies lost pet could be being used in this way, and that any poor stray dogs have to endure and suffer this torment, as if their lives haven't been hard enough already.

You can help though by visiting www.crueltyfreeinternational.org and sign their petition or even make a donation and together we can fight the good fight and try and end this global horror. Thank you.

You will never regret being kind

The Hedgehog

It was me that spotted him first, as I was lower to the
ground

Just lying there, not moving, not even mooching
around

I squealed, and I tugged on my lead ahead of
Mummy

I could sense he was hurt as he was still, lying on his
tummy

Mummy came running over to see what all the fuss
was about

It was then she started to worry and began to shout

"STAY" she ordered me, that's a poorly hog

We need to help him quick, and so she began to jog

She fetched a box and blanket and carefully placed
him in

It was then she saw the wound and knew it was grim

The poor hedgehog had been attacked by Magpies

And his breathing was very shallow

Mummy started to cry and said poor little fellow

We did what we could, and took him to the vet

That poor little hog, Mummy so upset

She cried and cried until we got home

So, I snuggled on her lap and got real, close

And told her she did more than most.

Rupert the Dog

October Birthday's & Important Date's

1st	19th
2nd	20th
3rd	21st
4th	22nd
5th	23rd
6th	24th
7th	25th
8th	26th
9th	27th
10th	28th
11th	29th
12th	30th
13th	31st
14th	
15th	
16th	
17th	
18th	

Sniffing

I stop to sniff everything

A lamppost, post box, even trees too

Nothing escapes, my nose is a weapon

I'm sniffing, I'm sniffing I'm dodging and steppin

A short walk can take me on a journey of senses

My body trembles as I stop and sniff fences

It's heaven for me to sniff poop and sniff wee

I then must stop and do a pee, pee

I am overloaded with many glorious smells

Fox, Cat, even humans too my nose compels

Back home now and time for some noms

As all those smells have tantalised my taste buds

Breakfast soon eaten, feel sleepy some more

I feel a snooze coming on, time for a snore

Rupert the Dog

November

Remember, Remember

Crisp, cold, damp dark nights, but on the fifth filled with frights

Loud bangs and whoosh sounds, right outside my window

It doesn't seem that anyone cares though

People rushing to a display, heads turned up to the night skies

Screams, shouts, the smell of smoke,

I hate it, though, it makes me choke

Cats, dogs even, rabbits too

Frightened, scared, what about the animals in the zoo

Stop and think this time of year

The heartache, the panic, the rising fear.

Fireworks, yes can be fun for some, but for most a pain in the bum

If you must crane your neck, then go to an organised event

And spare a thought for those that don't frequent.

Rupert the Dog

November, a month I personally hate, as it's when you idiot humans, in the U.K find it necessary to waste copious amounts of money, by setting off fireworks. No thought to us poor animals, who get frightened, no, you are all selfish bastards. Why you celebrate Guy Fawkes anyway is beyond me, he was just a terrorist, trying to blow up the Houses of Parliament!!

If you don't know the story of Guido "Guy" Fawkes, then let me educate you, perhaps then you will stop and think this year, "Do I really want to hurt Rupert"

Guy Fawkes along with his 12 co-conspirators, tried to assassinate King James I of England, by blowing up the Houses of Parliament with 36 barrels of gun powder. This was a planned act of terrorism to take place at the opening of Parliament on November 5 1605.

So the, the rhyme " Remember, remember the 5th of November", should not be celebrated with ear splitting, scary fireworks, which are made with explosives may I add, but surely you should all have a few minutes silence and NOT waste your money on those fucking big banging bombs celebrating a terrorist!!!!

However, if you are still going to be a twat and celebrate, then spare a thought for the elderly, and animals who get scared, also please can you check under bonfires, BEFORE YOU LIGHT THEM for hedgehogs as this time of year they will be looking for somewhere cosy and warm to hibernate, and you don't want to also be known for burning hogs alive, now do you!!!

"Fury Friends make the best companions, we will never lie to you or let you down"- Rupert the Dog

November Birthday's & Important Date's

1st		19th
2nd		20th
3rd		21st
4th		22nd
5th	Don't be a Twat	23rd
6th		24th
7th		25th
8th		26th
9th		27th
10th		28th
11th		29th
12th		30th
13th		
14th		
15th		
16th		
17th		
1		

December

GIN

That time again, has come too soon, presents, paper sends me into a loon

Oh what shall we get, Aunt Doris this year, and what about Nan

No slippers, I fear

The tree will go up maybe one week before, I shall try not to yell, as, it leans left of the door.

What shall we eat, it's the same every year, Turkey, Chicken,

Oh fuck it, just have beer

Who shall we invite on the main Christmas Day?

My Sister, Yours, what about Great Aunty Faye

There is only one thing for it, and that's crack open that gin

As Christmas was made for saying fuck it, it all goes in the bin

Rupert the Dog

The Tree

Oh, what is this I spy in the corner, a tree just for me?

How, lucky I am

It smells weird though, and has twinkly things

And something on top with what looks like wings!

Yes, it is green and looks real enough,

But it is leaning slightly and stuck in a bucket

I wander up to it, and I cock my leg,

Oooo the relief, now I won't need to wee in my bed

But I hear sizzling and now I see smoke,

Jesus Christ I am starting to choke

The twinkly things, have set on fire

Dear lord I think I am now really in the mire!

Rupert the Dog

Ho, Ho, Fucking HO! Well, where has that year gone, and what acts of kindness have you achieved throughout?

I know this time of year for some, can be a lonely time, and so please check on your neighbours, friends, if you have any, (not like my Aunty Jane) and any relatives, providing you like them that is!. Also make sure if it's cold you check on any animals too.

If like my Mummy, you love Christmas, then, you have to endure being sung at, stupid carols, which half the time she makes up, or sings, in an operatic voice! Oh and then there is the nostalgia, which doesn't last long with Dad, he is a right misery guts, Bah humbug, they don't even buy gifts anymore, they donate to charity and then buy scratch cards, which they then all take turns to rub off and see who wins, last year, Mummy won her money back ha-ha!!

The reason they stopped giving gifts, wasn't because Daddy is such a tight arse, no, it was because they have so much crap already that each year was the same, Mummy would get new pyjamas, perfume and a book, Daddy would get something horrendous, as Mummies gift buying skills are legendary!! I shall give you an example, if you don't believe me…

One year, Daddy asked for a CD (before, downloads and iPod) he wanted OMD (Orchestral Manoeuvre's in the Dark) and some new underpants, he never wants for much!! So Christmas morning came around, Mummy was her usual excitable self, chanting " He's Been" like she is 5 years old (idiot) and they sit down to open their presents.

Mummy got a gorgeous hat and scarf set, the book she wanted, perfume, and pjs, she was delighted, but what excited her the most was the giving and seeing Daddies face!!!

Daddy proceeded to open his presents, first underpants, there were like 20 pairs, and, looked to me like they wouldn't fit a fucking cat, let alone my Daddy, (he is on the chunky side) I started wheezing, trying to contain my laughter. Daddy held them up and said "what the fuck are these" and then read the label, made in China!! HA HA, Mummy had brought them off the local market stall, thinking she was getting a bargain,20 pairs for £15, all in array of garish colours, there were, neon yellow, orange, brown with a blue stripe, black with a yellow strip, those were my favourite as I thought Daddy could look like a giant bumble bee! And a hideous khaki green pair. Mummy said she thought they looked sturdy, and the brown ones, would hide a multitude of sins, whatever that meant, but she failed to notice she had picked up small, instead of large, so these were dumped in the bin (as apparently you can't return underwear).

Next came the CD, and I wish I could have captured the look on my Daddies face, it was priceless, kind of aghast mixed with shit on your shoe, it was the Greatest Hits, but not of OMD, no, it was ELO (Electric Light Orchestra) which Daddy hated. He couldn't work out, whether it was because Mummy, didn't know him, or she was just plain stupid!! I went with, she is just plain stupid. HA HA HA HA …… They still laugh about it to this day, I mean how on earth do you get those mixed up, Mummy said it was because she got confused with her alphabet!!! So, as you can see gift giving in our house has been somewhat amusing, and trust me it never got any better, so they decided to quit, less hassle, less stress and if either of them truly wanted something, they just would go out and buy it.

We also have to endure Mummies nostalgia, and yes, it is as bad as you think, she gets all gooey and stupid, and whimsical, Daddy laughs, and always says, what memory, are we recreating this year!! Again, there have been a few………..

One Christmas, we had NUTS!!! Mummy was having one of her nostalgic moments, and she said she remembered when she was little that what she loved about visiting her Grandad, (not potato) were the nuts in a bowl.

Her Grandad would be sat in his favourite armchair, braces on over his shirt, (men always wore braces then). He would have a large King Edward Cigar dangling from his lips, the smell was divine, and a cut glass with whiskey in it on the hearth. On a little table, which was always beside him, was the largest bowl of nuts you did see, and a solid metal nut cracker. He would sit the entire time she was there, just cracking nut after nut after nut, munching away, the shells being discarded up the fireplace, Mummy used to be mesmerised, and her Grandad always used to crack them with such ease. Occasionally, if you were lucky he would crack one for her, and oh the pleasure of eating a walnut, which always reminded her of two halves of a brain ha, was delicious.

NB; 70's kids did not have fucking nut allergies, never heard of, same as ADHD, if a kid was naughty, he was a fucking little cunt!

The walnut, tasted yummy and reminded her of the choc treat, called, walnut whip, which were a luxury to her back then and she used to get them for Christmas, and so to get given one of Grandad's nuts, to her was a real treat.

So, this one year, she went out and brought a massive bag of Brazil nuts, walnuts and hazelnut's and a nut cracker. She piled them high in the bowl and stood back to admire her handiwork. Dad on the other hand laughed and said, I bet you £10 they get chucked out and you don't eat fucking one.

Well, Christmas came, and Christmas went, and there on the dining table stood the bowl of fucking nuts, I will say this, she did try cracking several, but the useless cheap, wanker nut cracker, broke, or it may have been accidently smashed up the wall!! She said, it never seemed this much bother when Grandad was sat cracking them, and it all seemed too much of a fucking pain in the arse.

So the nuts all went in the bin, she was meant to give Dad £10 but told him he could whistle for it, and that was the end of that nostalgic moment. There have been many more, including, a real Christmas tree, which I nearly got crushed under, a wreath for the door, until it fell on Daddies head one night!! Snowballs, not actual, but an alcoholic beverage, that looked like someone had pissed and jizzed in a glass at the same time!! And last but not least paper chain decorations, around the fire, need I say more.......

December Birthday's & Important Date's

1st

2nd

3rd

4th

5th

6th

7th

8th

9th

10th

11th

12th

13th

14th

15th

16th

17th

18th

19th

20th

21st

22nd

23rd

24th

25th

26th

27th

28th

29th

30th

31st

And so, another year has come to an end, I hope it has been filled with happiness, prosperity and copious amounts of gin, I wish you all a very Merry Christmas and Happy New Year, if you haven't been kind, you will forever remain a twat.

Rupert the Dog

Thank you for buying my book, your generosity has helped sad animals at Wetnose Animals

15621388R00065

Printed in Great Britain
by Amazon